STOICISM

A PHILOSOPHICAL GUIDE TO LIFE, INCLUDING DIY-EXERCISES
ON PRACTICAL STOICISM FOR THE REALIZATION
OF LIFE'S ACTIONS

ROBERT GREEN

Stoicism

A Philosophical Guide to Life

Including DIY-Exercises on Practical Stoicism for the Realization of Life's Actions

By Robert Green

Stoicism:

A Philosophical Guide to Life

Including DIY-Exercises on Practical Stoicism for the Realization of our Life's Actions

Copyright © 2019 by Robert Green

Table of Contents

Introduction 9

Chapter 1: Stoicism- In a Nutshell...........11

Chapter 2: Stoicism on the Rise 14

Ancient Wisdom in Modern Times............ 14

Why Stoicism Helps Us 16

Chapter 3: The Chain to Action 21

Key Principles and the Stoic Mindset 21

Being aware 22

Every day is a dying day............................ 23

You don't own anything............................ 24

Don't overindulge.................................... 25

Stay in the present 26

Discipline matters 26

Count on yourself 27

The Stoic Goals and the Toolbox for a Good Life 28

What will Batman do? 29

Negative Visualization 30

Voluntary Discomfort 31

Add a Reserve Clause 32

Love your Fate... 33

Pain and Sickness.................................... 35

A Loan from Future 36

Always Count your Blessings..................... 37

Forgive Other's Wrongs............................ 38

Instead, Buy some Tranquility 40

Reflect Yourself 42

Chapter 4: The Realization of Our Life's Actions **44**

Chapter 4.1: Mastering yourself **44**

On taking the right perspective **44**
Instead of the issue, focus on the lesson 45
Positivity attracts positivity 47
Distance yourself from negativity 48
Reward yourself...48

On rendering the right judgment **50**

On controlling your emotions **54**
Don't react immediately 57
Seek guidance 58
Find an outlet 58
See the bigger picture...60
Thoughts matter 60

On forgiveness **61**

On coping with adversity............................ **63**
The right mindset 64
Don't make any excuses 65
Have some faith...66
Never take "no" for an answer 67
Let your success energize you...68

On the art of learning and changing.......... **69**

On clarity and awareness **76**
3 Why's... 77
Emotional vocabulary 78
Saying "No." 79
Visceral reactions 80

Your Flaws 80

Self-talk.. 81

Your body language 82

The Devil's advocate 82

Self-evaluation 83

Constructive feedback....................83

Improve mental clarity 84

Chapter 4.2: Mastering your surroundings **88**

On dealing with other people **88**

Never criticize.................................89

Be appreciative 90

Other's perspective 91

On thinking what others think **92**

Perspective 93

Question yourself 94

Perfectionism 94

Understand yourself 95

Your tribe..95

Vulnerabilities 95

On seeking fame **97**

On virtue and kindness **100**

Don't take it personally..................102

Has it harmed you?........................102

Don't respond to rudeness 103

On money and wealth **106**

Daily good habits 107

Create goals 107

Self-improvement 108

Your health matters 108

Relationships matter 109

Moderation 109
Get things done 110
Positivity 110

On luxurious living 112

Your schedule 113
Go tech-free 113
Bad habits 114
Buy something...114
Healthy living 115

Chapter 4.3: Facing the Evening of Life. 116

On becoming old 116

Set realistic expectations 117
Relax a little 118
Don't be in denial 118
Attractiveness 119
Don't live in your past 119
Be proud and grateful 120

On losing control 121

What can you control? 122
Your Fears... 123
Your influence 124
Contemplation vs. problem-solving 124
Healthy affirmations 125

On facing mortality 127

Paperwork... 128
Mindfulness 128
Discuss death... 129
Good death 129

On acceptance.. 131

On meditation.. 133

Conclusion...................................... *136*

Introduction

I want to thank you for choosing this book, Stoicism: A Philosophical Guide to Life - Including DIY-Exercises on Practical Stoicism for the Realization of Life's Actions.'

Stoicism is neither an old nor an outdated philosophy like most people seem to think. This is one philosophy that is as relevant today as it was in the past. It is practical and is designed to work well in the real world by offering guidance and practical advice that people have been using for more than 2000 years.

In this book, you will learn about stoicism and how you can incorporate it into your daily life. It will help you become calmer, kinder, control your emotional volatility, help you overcome any adversities in life while holding onto your inner peace and prepares you to meet life without getting overwhelmed. The Stoic exercises mentioned in this book are not only easy but are practical as well.

It is time that you reap all these benefits and

start enjoying and living your life instead of just surviving. So, if you are ready to learn more about this ancient philosophy, let's start!

Chapter 1: Stoicism- In a Nutshell

This book is a practical guide on how you can embrace a Stoic lifestyle. All the exercises mentioned in this book are quite simple and practical.

The philosophy of stoicism is designed such that it encourages and helps people to lead the best version of their life. It is a philosophy that actively tries to optimize the positive emotions you experience while minimizing any negative ones and thereby helping you to hone your character.

Stoicism provides the skeletal framework essential to lead a good life regardless of where you are at life. Stoicism was created deliberately to understand life and come up with actionable goals that are practical and attainable.

These days, it feels like stoicism is having a renaissance in the modern world. From politicians to entrepreneurs and everyone else in between seems fascinated with the concept of stoicism.

Stoicism is an ancient philosophy that can be traced back to ancient Greece and Rome during the early parts of the 3rd Century BC. It is quintessential that you keep in mind that the thought process was quite different back then. The primary concern for many was to avoid leading an unfortunate life. Therefore, they were more interested in doing things, thinking such thoughts and behaving in such a manner that will increase their satisfaction in life. You must remember that in the ancient world, no one automatically assumed that by earning money and acquiring materialistic things, they will gain happiness. At that time, all those people simply desired to find a way in which they can have an excellent soul.

Stoicism is a popular school of thought that managed to answer compelling questions related to anxiety, fear, stress, the meaning of life, and the purpose of life. The answer to all this was that you must lead a virtuous life to attain happiness and tranquility in life.

For instance, a person can hone their virtues by

giving more importance to their deeds instead of their words. Stoicism is based on the belief that positive behavior helps create a positive life experience and vice versa. This school of thinking prescribes a particular way of thinking and living. The primary focus of stoicism is on leading a virtuous life, on finding happiness and reducing any negative emotions.

The most important Stoic thinkers are Marcus Aurelius, Lucius Annaeus Seneca, Zeno Citium and Epictetus.

Chapter 2: Stoicism on the Rise

Ancient Wisdom in Modern Times

Different philosophies from all over the world like stoicism and Zen still make sense today like they did when they were introduced and we are in dire need of these philosophies today more than ever.

The Socratic method of inquiry encourages us to question everything including ourselves. This line of thought encourages freethinking and enables one to cultivate his or her own beliefs. It also encourages critical thinking. Plato's allegory of the cave introduced the concepts of an ideal republic and the way humans turn a blind eye towards truth. His thinking encourages people to let go of their ignorance and start actively seeking the truth. It encourages people to live in and accept the reality of the world instead of living in blissful ignorance. Aristotle strongly believed that the world is made of facts and to gain knowledge, one needs to apply logic and use methodical discourse. This line of thinking is applicable in all aspects of life. Almost all ancient philosophies encourage people to seek happiness. For instance, stoicism is all about keeping your cool even in chaos, and to lead a fruitful life. A powerful proponent of stoicism is about making us better human beings. It also encourages people to live in the moment, embrace their true selves and always value inner peace more than any other materialistic possession of this world.

The teachings of Zen philosophy encourage the followers to live in the moment, enjoy and cherish the present, to believe that happiness is closer than we seem to think and to enjoy the process of life. It encourages people to actively look for solutions to their problems instead of concocting the worst possible outcomes.

Why Stoicism Helps Us

Values → Mindset → Goals → Tools → Actions

With stoicism, you can uncover your real values and learn about the things that do matter to you instead of going with what others seem to believe. Once you know your values, you can try to develop an ideal mindset to live by your values and try to uphold them. Your values help you determine your goals. If you don't have any goals in life, you merely exist and aren't living. Your goals give you the necessary strength and motivation to keep going even when things get difficult. Once you know your goals, you can use the relevant tools to achieve those goals. You will learn about the tools that you can use in the next chapter. The final step is to start taking action to attain your goals and to uphold your values. You will learn all about this in the final chapter in this book.

In this section, you will learn about the reasons why stoicism is not only still relevant today but is extremely helpful as well.

Stoicism was practiced in the age of the

gladiators, so how can it possibly be still relevant today? The wisdom of this ancient philosophy isn't time-barred, and it's a quest for happiness, and the key to a meaningful existence is now more necessary than ever. The stoic philosophy helps find answers to questions about life that other traditional schools don't talk about. You might learn about a lot of things in your school and college, but you don't learn about certain important things like how to deal with the challenges that life throws your way.

How do you face your fears? How do you overcome any adversities? How do you come to terms with mortality? How do you deal with your emotions and other equally important questions? Stoicism helps answer all this and even provides you with the necessary tools to turn your life around.

The stoic philosophy is quite different than any other conventional school of thinking. It helps you understand that true happiness lies within and isn't dictated by your external success. Instead of focusing on materialistic things, it encourages the person to focus on himself. At the end of the day, who you are and what you do matters way more than what you own.

We all like to believe that we can control everything, but the reality is that we can hardly control anything. Stoicism helps you to accept what happens and come to terms with the fact that the only thing you can control is the way you react to situations. You cannot control the outcomes for events in your life or how others are to you, but you can control the way you respond to all this. By focusing on what you can control instead of all that you cannot, you can overcome stress and anxiety.

It helps you understand that you are the only one responsible for your life. Your character, the choices you make and the way you act shape your life and no one else is responsible. If you let someone bother you, it is because you are giving him or her that permission to bother you.

Stoicism offers practical guidance about life and how to deal with it. Also, it is science-friendly. The techniques used by Stoics are almost the same as the ones that are proven to be true by modern research in today's concept of positive psychology. Stoicism isn't rigid but is open to interpretation.

Here is the chain of action that stoicism uses:

Values→ Mindset→ Goals→ Tools→ Actions

In this world that we live in which is overwrought with information, it can be quite confusing. There are so many world views, various religious directions, numerous beliefs and philosophies and so on. All of this can be quite overwhelming. Stoicism provides a clear set of values that will help you understand your mindset.

Your values influence your mindset. What you believe will certainly affect the way you think. Once you start thinking clearly with the help of stoicism, you will be able to come up with goals for yourself. Goals are quintessential for succeeding in life. If you have the necessary goals in mind, you can focus on gathering all of the necessary tools (knowledge in this instance) and then use it to attain your goals.

So, the final step is action. In a world where plenty of information is available freely, such information simply becomes worthless. The only thing that's more precious than

information is the information that has been
successfully converted into actionable goals.
Knowledge is certainly powerful, but the
knowledge that's been implemented in more
powerful.

Chapter 3: The Chain to Action

Key Principles and the Stoic Mindset

In this section, you will learn about the essential principles that all Stoics follow. Following these principles will help you establish an ideal Stoic mindset.

Values→ Mindset→ Goals→ Tools→ Actions

This is precisely the direction that the Stoic philosophy flows in. Once you are aware of your values, you will be able to understand your mindset. Only if you understand yourself will you be able to determine realistic goals in life. Once you have your goals ready, you will need tools to take the necessary action. You will learn about the tools you can use and the actions you can take in the coming sections.

Being aware

Self-awareness is one of the most basic principles of stoicism, and it is quintessential to thrive in this world. You must be aware of the world around you as well as your yourself.

"You must get used to inspecting your thoughts, so that when someone asks you, 'What are you thinking about?' you must be able to readily respond."- Aurelius

So, how can you practice this principle? To fully understand yourself, you must learn to live in the present. While focusing on who you were and will be, you must also focus on who you are at present. Focus and concentration are essential to understand yourself. Make it a practice to only concentrate on one thing at a time. Notice the way your breath, your posture, the way your feet move and so on. Just try to take all this in and notice how you feel.

Every day is a dying day

"We all tend to live like we will all live forever, no conscious thought of your frailty ever comes to your mind and of all the time that's have gone by. We squander away our precious time as if it is available in abundant supply, though all the time that you spend on something or someone might be your last one."- Seneca

The sand continues to slip through the hourglass regardless of whether you are paying any attention to it or not. You never know when your life might come to an abrupt end. So, what's the point in squandering away your life on things and people who don't matter? Once you accept this, it can be quite liberating but also a little grim. The world will not stop spinning. So, take action today and start doing things that value and matter to you. Self-consciousness is perhaps the most selfish trait there is. Stop trying to look pretty for someone, stop trying to please others and instead start to live the way you want. In a bid to not offend anyone, most of us don't take the chances that we must. If you keep doing this, what will you receive in the end? Nothing. You would have lived a life that probably pleases others, but you haven't done anything that pleases yourself!

You must start behaving like there is no limit to your potential and that nothing is ever closed off to you. You will certainly come across certain things that you cannot do, but this way of thinking will be quite liberating.

You don't own anything

Make peace with the fact that you don't own anything. Everything that you have has been given to you by fortune. What fortune bestows on you can also be taken away. Don't get attached to material things. Instead, learn to cherish and enjoy things while you still have them instead of thinking of them as personal investments. You cannot make room for new things in life if you hold onto everything that comes your way.

Don't overindulge

"You must reject the pleasures of life because they make you soft and weak. Indulgences are demanding, and this prompts us to make insistent demand on Fortune."- Seneca

Pleasure is certainly nice and adding a little spice does make the steak tasty. However, overindulgence is not a pleasure and is a destructive trait. The world is quite literally at our fingertips these days, and one doesn't have to go through any struggle to acquire things. You might think that living like this has no consequences, but it does. When you get too used to the comforts of life and what you gain, you tend to lose things that matter. You slowly lose the ability to grow and develop. You need to stumble and fall a couple of times to grow in life truly. If you always opt for the "easiest way out" you will miss out on important things in life. Doing what is easy is certainly appealing, but think about whether it does anything for your growth or not.

Stay in the present

"Life can be quite short and anxious for all those who forget about the past, neglect their present and worry about the future. When their time comes to an end, the poor souls realize that it is too late for them and that they have spent all their time doing nothing!"- Seneca

In your life, all that you have is the moment you are living in. You cannot change the past and thinking about it will fill you with regret. You don't know how the future will pan out, so thinking about it will only fill you up with anxiety. So, learn to live in the moment. Whenever you are doing something, ensure that you are doing it wholeheartedly and you will not have the time to worry about the things you cannot control.

Discipline matters

One trait that everyone desires is self-discipline. Discipline refers to the ability to follow through on something you say that you will do, even when you don't feel like doing it.

Self-discipline is the key to personal development. It takes discipline to face challenges in life without giving up. It is essential in all aspects of your life. For instance, you might start a new diet and exercise regime, and there will be times when you will want to give up. In such instances, you need the discipline to ensure that you stick to your plans.

Count on yourself

Self-reliance is one of the fundamental concepts of stoicism. You are the only one you can truly rely on. You might have a lot of friends, but will they live your life for you? Will they do your work for you? You are the only one that can take yourself from point X to Y. They might be able to lead you to water, but you are the only one that can drink! You must embrace the fact that you are the only one that's responsible for all your actions. You might or might not have caused something, but you are responsible for the way you react. You don't need a knight in shining armor to come to your rescue; you are your hero! You will learn about various tools that will come in handy later on in this book.

The Stoic Goals and the Toolbox for a Good Life

"There is a reason why philosophers often warn that one must never be satisfied with learning but need to practice it as well. As times goes by, we tend to forget all that we learned and end up doing the exact opposite of it, and form opinions that are opposite of what one should."
-Epictetus

Why is LeBron James exceptional? That's because he trains daily and that's the main reason. You become good at something only if you practice it often. You need to train hard and keep practicing. This applies to all aspects of life. Practice the stoic exercises, and you will get better at living your life. It all boils down to what you do and not what you know. This is one philosophy that all stoics live by. LeBron is amongst the best basketball players, but he still practices. It is not because he doesn't know how to play; it is just to make himself good at what he does. Likewise, your job doesn't end with reading these stoic exercises; instead, you need to practice them if you want to turn your life around. Here are the different exercises that you can practice.

What will Batman do?

"You must choose a person whose way of living as well as words have gained your approval. Always point that person out to yourself either as your guardian or as your idol. According to me, there is a need to set someone else as a standard against your character so that you can measure yourself. You cannot make a crooked line straight if you don't have a ruler"-Seneca

The Stoic sage is someone who is considered to be a supreme being - the perfect human being. The Stoic sage is a completely virtuous and is a good person who leads a smooth and happy life. She is the hypothetical and ideal role model according to stoicism. Since the Stoic sage isn't someone you are close with, let me give you another example. Let us consider Batman to be a role model. When you apply this philosophy to a situation, you must ask yourself what Batman would do if he were in your situation? You can change this according to the situations

- "what would an ideal boss do?" or "what would the perfect friend do in this situation?"

Negative Visualization

"We must always project our thoughts ahead of us at every turn and consider all the possible outcomes in a situation instead of just the usual events that take place"- Seneca

In negative visualization, you need to imagine all the probably worst-case scenarios in your head so that you will be prepared whenever they occur and will be able to stay in control. All this helps you react desirably and helpfully. If something catches you by surprise, it hurts a lot more than something that you are prepared for. This is the main reason why you need to try and see the things coming your way. If you know that someone is about to punch you, it might hurt, but it also helps you take certain steps to reduce the pain you feel.

For this exercise, you need to take some time and think about all the probable unfortunate events that might occur. Do you have anything coming up like an exam, a meeting, a presentation or anything else? Once you have a situation in mind, think about the things that can go wrong. Think about your loved ones and what you will feel if they disappeared? How will you react in such a situation? Consider your beliefs about your mortality, what if you were to die right now? What are the feelings that this thought triggers within you?

Voluntary Discomfort

"Set a couple of days aside, and during these days, you must be content with the cheapest fare, with coarse and rough clothing, saying to yourself "is this the situation that scared me?" Your soul will strengthen itself only in such situations, and it will help you be prepared for situations of greater stress in the future. If you don't want to flinch in the time of crisis, then you need to prepare yourself for it before it comes." – Seneca

This exercise is about training and preparing yourself for uncomfortable situations so that you don't flinch even when they come around. This is about learning to get used to being uncomfortable to grow into your comfort zone. For instance, let us assume that you aren't comfortable with the idea of fasting for half a day. If you start practicing 24-hour fast once a week, you will be comfortable with the idea of fasting for half a day at a stretch, and it will become quite easy.

You need to place yourself in uncomfortable situations intentionally. There are different ways in which you can do this. Try to sleep on the floor once or twice a week or skip drinking coffee for a week.

Add a Reserve Clause

"If nothing obstructs me, I will sail across the ocean." – Seneca

All stoics know they cannot control everything. So, they add a reserve clause to all their actions. A stoic will try to do everything that they possibly can if nothing obstructs them. Adding a reserve clause to your actions is a way of reminding yourself of all the uncertainties of life. You never know what the future holds in store for you. That's the reason why Muslims use the phrase "inshallah" whenever they talk about something good, it means "If God is willing." This way of thinking is twofold, and it states that one must try to do their very best to succeed while accepting that the outcome is never under one's control. So, whenever you are doing something you need to add a reserve clause to it that states, "If nothing prevents or obstructs me." For instance, I will finish writing this article by tonight, if nothing prevents me from doing this. Or "I will meet you for dinner, inshallah."

Love your Fate

"Fate will always lead the willing and drag along all those who are reluctant."- Seneca

Stoics follow the principle of Amor fati or love your fate. Stoics know that fate is something that's beyond one's control. So, they believe that instead of wishing for the reality to be something different, they merely need to accept and love it as is. A common metaphor used in stoicism is that of a dog leashed to a moving cart. A wise man is like a dog that's chained to a moving cart, running along happily with the cart and keeping pace with it, whereas a foolish person is like a grumpy dog that struggles with the leash and finds itself being dragged with it instead of moving alongside it.

You cannot change all the things that happen to you in life. So, it is a good idea to accept this fact instead of fighting it. We are all like dogs that are chained to a cart - we are all free up to the extent that the leash lets us. Therefore, it is up to you whether you want to enjoy this journey, or you want to get dragged along with it.

Whenever something happens to you, take a moment and think about whether you can do anything about it or not. If not, then understand that fate controls it. Fighting it is a sheer waste of your time and energy, and it will make you feel miserable. So, instead learn to accept it. You must not wish for the reality to be anything different than what it is and don't judge events, instead learn to accept them. Everything is a learning experience, try not to repeat your mistakes and work hard. These are the only things that you can control, the sooner you accept it, the easier your life will be.

Pain and Sickness

"Diseases is an obstruction to the body and not your will. For instance, lameness impedes the limb but not the will. You need to use this reflection while dealing with everything that happens- you will notice that an impediment is to something else but never to yourself."- Epictetus

Epictetus was lame, but he chose to believe that it was merely an impediment to his leg but not his mind. This holds for physical pain and sickness of the body. The pain and discomfort are impediments to the body and not the mind. You always have the option of how you want to deal with it. If you have a terrible headache, you can either choose to bear it, or you can whine about it. This choice is entirely up to you. This exercise in stoicism is about overcoming your weakness and not letting it control your life. The next time you feel any physical discomfort or pain, you need to train your virtue and remember that the discomfort is only physical and not mental. If you have a fever, you must rest instead of complaining about it. Try not to let the pain bother you and instead strive to preserve your inner peace.

A Loan from Future

"We don't have any basis to indulge in self-admiration, as though we are all surrounded by possessions that are loaned to us. We are free to use and enjoy them, but the giver of these gifts decides the tenancy. In the meanwhile, we are duty bound to take care of these gifts and keep them ready for a return as and when they are called upon without making a squeak. Only a sorry debtor abuses his creditor."- Seneca

The only thing that is truly ours is our mind, and everything else can be taken away. Possessions, your body, family, friends and everything else can be taken away from you within the blink of an eye. According to the stoic philosophy, you need to learn to enjoy all the things that you do have for as long as possible without getting attached to them. Think of everything around you as something that you have borrowed from the future. So, everything is temporary, and it can be taken away without prior notice. It is nothing but sheer ignorance to think that no misfortune can befall you when you see all the misfortune happening in the world around you.

A simple exercise that you can do to adopt stoicism is to constantly remind yourself that everything that you believe to be yours is not yours - even if you paid for it, it can be taken away from you. The sooner you accept this; the simpler life will be for you.

Always Count your Blessings

"You must never set your mind on things that you don't possess and believe that they are yours. Instead, learn to count your blessings and be grateful for all that you possess and think about how much you might desire them if such things were truly yours. However, watch yourself so that you don't get too attached to them that it will trouble you to lose them."- Aurelius

The Stoics were all staunch minimalists. They knew that it was better to cherish all that they had instead of pining for something they didn't. They were grateful for all that they had going in their lives. Stoics believe that it is better to want the things that they have, instead of desiring the things that they didn't. Essentially, they fought their urge to horde things, cherished what they had and never got attached to the things they possessed because things can be taken away at the snap of a finger.

This exercise is quite simple. If you didn't have the things that you did, then how much will you wish for them? Like with all the previous exercises, you need to make a list of things. For instance, you need to make a list of three things that you are grateful for in your life.

You don't have to buy things that you don't need. You need to be grateful for the things that you do have, and you must not get attached to the things that you cherish.

Forgive Other's Wrongs

"Whenever a person assents, to something that isn't true, know that the said person did not wish to assent to something untrue- Like Plato said that 'for no soul on earth is robbed of the truth without its consent.' But for the fact that it seemed true to that person."- Epictetus

The Stoics understood that all that everyone tries to do is what they think is right even when it isn't so. People don't do something wrong intentionally; they only act because they think it is right and you must learn to pity them instead of blaming them for their actions. Being angry with someone who didn't know any better is a waste of time. So, you must learn to be kind and tolerant towards them instead of getting angry or bitter. You need to learn to forgive others of their wrongs. Before you get upset with someone, take some time and tell yourself that the said person didn't know any better. If you do this, you will be kind and forgiving towards that person instead of being bitter. After all, humans tend to make mistakes, and that's a basic human trait.

You must not seek revenge because it stems from weakness. Instead, be tolerant towards them. Instead of being upset, learn to pity the wrongdoers because they didn't know any better and were blinded by their minds. If someone was mean to you, then think of it as a learning experience. Shake it off and get on with your life instead of wasting your time harboring any negative emotions.

Instead, Buy some Tranquility

"Start with things that aren't valuable - a portion of spilled milk or stolen wine- repeat this statement to yourself- 'that's a small price to pay to buy some tranquility and peace of mind.'"- Epictetus

This line of thought is sheer genius. A goal for all stoics is the ability to stay calm in the face of unfavorable circumstances. Regardless of what a stoic face, he or she will want to stay calm and rational. The sentence "I choose to buy peace of mind instead" can save you from squandering your energy and emotions. Usually, if something that you don't like happens to you, then you will experience a volley of negative emotions. All such emotions will disturb your inner peace and make you irritable. Instead, let it go and do so with a smile. This is one of the best stoic philosophies that you can incorporate into your life. The only condition to apply this is that you need sufficient awareness to be able to step in between the negative stimulus and your response. If you can work this distinction out, you will benefit from it.

This stoic practice works something like this - you need to opt for awareness in your life, and whenever something upsetting happens, you must tell yourself "instead of the negative emotions, I want to buy some tranquility."

For instance, if you spill wine over your favorite dress, instead of getting upset about it, you need to opt to buy some tranquility instead. If you are calm and rational, you can find a way to fix this problem. When your partner doesn't do the dishes like promised, instead of picking a fight, opt for tranquility. If you are calm, you can discuss with your partner about the things that upset you, and you can work out a solution. Loss of mental peace is the worst thing that you can do to yourself. Your inner sense of tranquility is something that you can control.

Reflect Yourself

"Don't go to sleep unless you reflect upon all that you did during the day. Take some time to critically analyze your day- what are the things that you did wrong? What can you do to fix those mistakes? And why did I do what I did? All these questions will help you review your acts, improve yourself and rejoice in the acts that you did well."- Epictetus

The question you must ask yourself before you drift off to sleep is "Which of the exercises did I implement today?"

You need to start somewhere, and there is no time like the present to get started. All the exercises mentioned in this chapter are simple and helpful, but they need some practice. You cannot perfect something without practice, and the same applies to these exercises as well. You don't need anyone else to check on you, and you can do it by yourself. You need to spend a couple of minutes reflecting on your day. Think about all the things that you did, whether you have made any progress or not, what are the things that you are doing well and what are the things that you need to improve upon? Such daily reflections will help you have more productive days and will also help improve your awareness.

Here are three questions that you must ask yourself before you sleep: "Did I do any good today?" "What can I do better if I had a chance to redo it? And "What steps do I need to take to be the best that I can be?"

Now that you are aware of the different exercises you can follow; the next step is to start applying them in real life. Your job doesn't end with reading, but the actual job starts once you complete reading about these stoic exercises. The simple truth is that the way physical exercises improve your physical strength, practicing mental exercises will help strengthen your mind.

Chapter 4: The Realization of Our Life's Actions

Your life is all about the way you act or react to situations that come along your way. In this chapter, you will learn about different ways in which you can master yourself, master your surroundings and tips to face the evening of your life successfully.

Chapter 4.1: Mastering yourself

On taking the right perspective

"The happiness of the life you lead solely depends on the quality of thoughts you entertain."- Aurelius

Having the right perspective in life makes all the difference. If you perceive something to be unfavorable regardless of whether it is good or not, it will always elicit negative emotions in your mind. Stoics believed that life was all about perspective and once you manage to have the right perspective in life; you will be able to do well for yourself. For instance, if you view misfortune as punishment, all that you will do is resent it; instead, if you view it as a learning experience, you will be able to learn something from even all those situations that you viewed as "negative or bad" in your life.

In this section, you will learn about a couple of simple steps that you can follow to ensure that you always have the right perspective in life.

Instead of the issue, focus on the lesson

This is certainly easier said than done. Good as well as bad experiences are a part of life, and we cannot control them. The one thing that you must never forget is that all experiences are good ones. You must try to find the silver lining. I am not implying that all events are good, but what you think or how you perceive them is what matters. There is always a scope to change and evolve. All that you must do is take a closer look at a situation, and you can find the silver lining. For instance, if you are passed over for a much-anticipated promotion at work, the chances are that you will feel quite disappointed. You might even want to quit, instead of doing this, carefully analyze what went wrong. You might not have been as effective at work as you probably assumed, or you might need to improve certain aspects of your work ethics. You can either do this or wallow in self-pity. If you opt for the former then you can evolve, but if you opt for the latter then all it results in is a waste of your time. Instead of thinking that you were wronged, try to think "I now have the knowledge, so I can find the right tools to find a solution."

Developing this sort of a positive perspective doesn't happen overnight, and you must practice this skill daily. What this example shows is that you can take every problem that you face in life and think of it as an opportunity for growth. Remember that everything that happens, happens for a reason. You can either go along with your fate on a joyous journey, or you can be dragged along. It is entirely up to you what you want to do.

Positivity attracts positivity

You smile, and the world will smile with you. Now that you know the importance of gratitude, being grateful daily will make you feel more positive. Here is a simple exercise that you must start practicing. You can either do this at night or as soon as you wake up. You must ask yourself about the three things that you are grateful for or the three things that make you happy. By doing this, you are essentially programming your mind to focus on all things good while ignoring any negative thoughts. Being grateful is a great way to boost positivity, and positivity attracts more positivity in your life.

The more you focus on doing things that make you happy, the happier you will be. Positive emotions attract more positive emotions, and negative ones attract negative ones. So, if you want to get rid of all things negative, then try to focus on the good things in your life or the things that make you happy.

Distance yourself from negativity

If you can distance yourself from all negativity, it increases the scope of attracting more positivity into your life. If you feel that something or someone is purely toxic in your life, then you need to distance yourself from it. You must understand that you neither have the time nor space for negativity. It is all about changing your perspective in life. For instance, if you are in a relationship with someone who is extremely controlling and doesn't let you grow or think freely, then the best thing that you can do is to end that toxic relationship. You must discard everything that doesn't add any positivity to your life.

Reward yourself

The first positive action that you have already taken is to go through this section to become a better version of yourself. Come on, pat yourself on the back, you deserve it. It is not only important to change the way you think, but it is equally important to reward yourself whenever you do something that's desirable according to you. Accepting and embracing a change in your thoughts and perspective isn't something easy. You will not be able to change yourself overnight, and that process will take some time and energy. But that doesn't mean that you don't acknowledge your efforts for trying to make that change. Your life is all about perception. A simple change in the way you look at life can turn things around for you. If you want to focus on negativity, then everything that comes your way will feel negative to you, and all this negativity will bog you down.

A simple exercise that you can do is apply the "love your fate" tool of stoicism and reflect on your experience. Apply this technique to understand that there will always be things that you cannot control. All that you can do is try to learn from your experiences. If you want to learn to master yourself, then you need to work on adopting the right perspective. Make a note of your observations here.

On rendering the right judgment

"The soul is often dyed with the colors of one's thoughts"- Aurelius

Most of us tend to judge others based on what we seem to think is the truth. The truth is a mere perception, and it can change based on your perception of things and facts.

Some words like judgment tend to carry just and unjust implications. In the legal system, we all look up to the judges to uphold the law, but that doesn't mean that we like to appear before a judge, even a highly qualified one. However, no one likes to be judged by others. So, if you don't like being judged, then you must make it a point not to judge others.

Well, that's how it must be, but sadly it isn't. We are all quite judgmental - intentionally or unintentionally. Did you ever say that someone was a bad driver, a horrible cook or maybe a lousy manager? If you did, then that was a judgment you doled out about someone else. This sort of judgment isn't certainly nice, and it can affect someone else's career or even livelihood. For instance, if you are a manager, then the decisions you make about hiring, promoting or even giving a raise to an employee are all based on your judgment. We are all making hundreds of judgments daily, and they all guide you in your life. I believe that you will embrace this simple fact and try do everything that you can to become aware of all these judgments and then decide in an unbiased manner. All this might seem quite complicated. At times you might think that you are making a decision based on facts whereas there might be some unconscious bias that affects your choice.

It doesn't mean that you must never make any decisions; it merely means that you must make decisions rationally and cautiously.

Before you decide anything, ask yourself "Do I have all the facts or do I think that I have all the facts?" "Is there something that I am missing?" "Have I considered everything there is?" and once you do this, go back and reconsider all your answers once again.

You can ask others for their opinions about what they would do if they were in your shoes. You must not rely on their opinions, but you can certainly consider them before you decide anything. A little extra input when in a tough spot certainly helps.

You must realize the effect of your judgment as well. Does it affect you and anyone else? You must remind yourself of all those times when your judgment served you quite well. This helps develop the necessary confidence to trust yourself.

Once you make a decision, don't flip-flop. For instance, if you want to try a vegan diet, then please go ahead and try it for yourself and don't let any external opinion change your mind. Decide whether you like it or not after you try and not before.

Judgment is a skill that takes a lot of practice to master. You must start practicing on little things. You can do this with things like the clothes you buy or even when ordering something at a restaurant. These are all small judgment calls, but it prepares you to make bigger ones in the future.

You must never judge anyone else to make yourself feel better. Don't judge anyone and never put anyone down to make yourself feel superior. Learn to be compassionate while judging others. As I have mentioned, do you like being judged? If you don't, then what makes you think that you have any right to judge others?

A simple way in which you can hone your judgment-making skills is by meditating. The time spent meditating will help you get rid of any external beliefs and allows you to examine your decision and its consequences.

Use the "What will Batman do?" exercise in

Stoicism before you render any judgment and make a note of your experience here.

Notes:

____

____

____

____

____

____

____

____

___

On controlling your emotions

"You must frame your thoughts in such a manner that you are no longer enslaved by them so that you are no longer a puppet whose strings are controlled by impulses and you will stop complaining about all that's good in the present and stop dreading what lies in the future."- Aurelius

You must understand that there are a lot of things in this world and the life that you cannot control. You cannot control how others respond to you, what the future holds for you or how things turn out, but the one thing that you can control is the way you react to the circumstances in your life. You can always control the way you handle your emotions. The sooner you realize that you can control your emotions, the easier your life will be. You must never let your emotions control you, once they do, you will lose all sense of control. For instance, if you and your spouse have an argument and you carry that anger to a meeting or your work, I am certain that it will not do you any good. You will end up having an unproductive day. To avoid all this, you must learn to control your emotions.

Emotions are ceaseless, and at times they can be quite pressing and even a painful force that guides us. We might not want to believe it, but most of us are driven by our emotions. We tend to take a chance because a new prospect excites us. We tend to cry when someone hurts us, and we also make sacrifices for the ones we love. So, it is safe to say that emotions not only dictate our thoughts, but they also affect our actions and intentions. Usually, emotions replace rational thinking, and this can be quite troublesome. When you act on your emotions quickly, and if they turn out to be the wrong kind of emotions, then we make mistakes that we regret. Our feelings often oscillate between dangerous extremes. If you steer too far to the left, you are left with murderous rage and on the other end of the spectrum is euphoria. Well, like with any other aspect of your life, emotions need some moderation too. Emotions are good, but they must never replace logical thinking and rational perspective. That doesn't mean that you must not fall in love or do things spontaneously at times. All this is good, but negative emotions must be dealt with extreme caution.

Several of the negative emotions like envy, anger or even bitterness are capable of spinning out of control, especially in the instance when they are triggered. In time, if you aren't cautious, then these emotions grow like wild weeds that will dominate your life. Have you ever come across someone who seems to be in a constant state of anger? They certainly weren't born like that but they allowed certain unnecessary emotions fester and what you see now is the result of all those mismanaged emotions. So, how can you control your emotions and prevent the wrong type of emotions from governing your life? In this section, you will learn about six simple steps that will help you control your emotions.

Don't react immediately

A common mistake that a lot of people make is that they instantly react to an emotional trigger. If you do this, then you will certainly say or do something that you will regret. Before you give in to the urge to react to an emotional trigger, you must take a moment and stabilize your thoughts. Take a deep breath or count to ten to control the overwhelming need to react. Continue to keep taking deep breaths for a couple of minutes, and you can feel your body relax. Once your body relaxes, and your heart isn't fluttering away, things will become clear and calm.

Seek guidance

Faith is certainly our saving grace. Regardless of your age, sex, creed or any other demographic factor, it is a good idea to stay in touch with your spiritual self. You can always ask for divine guidance in times when you feel like you aren't able to control anything. When stuck in a sticky situation, try to think of a way out of it and ask the universe to help you find the right path.

Find an outlet

Now that you have successfully managed your emotions, you must not bottle it up, and you need to find a healthy outlet for it. If you keep your emotions bottled up for too long, then it will all burst out one fine day, and the sight certainly will not be pretty. The simplest thing you can do in such situations is to call up a friend or meet someone you trust and recount the entire incident to them. Once you start narrating the incident, you will probably realize that it was quite trivial or that you did a good thing by not reacting immediately. Also, when you hear someone else's opinion, it puts things in perspective and improves your awareness. If you aren't able to do this, then keep a journal with you. Make a note of all the things that were bothering you or left you feeling unsettled. As soon as you voice your thoughts or write them down, things will seem simpler to you. You can also go for a jog or a run to get rid of any negative emotions that were plaguing you. If possible, try to put some physical distance between yourself and the place that triggered such negative emotions. Some people find it helpful to turn to vigorous exercises like boxing or martial arts to displace their feelings whereas some turn to meditation. You can do anything that you like, as long as it helps you remove the negative emotions. When you don't react immediately, you give yourself some time to think things through. You will also be able to recognize certain things that escaped your notice the first time around.

See the bigger picture

Everything that happens in your life, all the good and the bad is all part of a bigger picture. Wisdom helps you see the bigger picture. If you react immediately, you lose perspective, and you fail to see what is in store for you. For instance, if you were passed over for a much deserving promotion, then perhaps it was an opportunity for you to learn some new skill or maybe you weren't ready for it. Don't let your emotions govern all your actions. Emotions are fleeting and what felt right once can seem wrong in the next moment.

Thoughts matter

Negative emotions come from negative thoughts. The more negative thoughts you entertain, the more negativity you will fester in your life. A simple way to break free of this vicious cycle is by replacing your thoughts. For instance, if you think that you hate someone and keep thinking about all the wrongs the said person did, the next time you meet them you will be hostile! Well, instead of doing this, try to replace your negative thoughts with positive ones. Always keep in mind that you don't know all the details. You must not jump to any hasty conclusions in an emotional state. Every cloud has a silver lining, and you merely need to find that in all situations.

On forgiveness

You must learn to forgive your emotional triggers. Your emotional trigger can be anyone - a friend, a family member, yourself or all of the above. You might experience sudden anger when your partner "does that thing he does," or experience a sense of self-loathing when you remember something that you did in the past and now regret. Well, mistakes are bound to happen, and no one is perfect. We all have flaws, and the only way to get on with life is to forgive all your emotional triggers. When you hold onto a grudge or any negative emotion, all the negativity will overwhelm you. However, when you learn to forgive, you can finally let go of the resentment, hatred, jealousy, anger or any other undesirable emotion and move ahead in life.

When you don't control your emotions, and you let them control you, you are heading towards a lot of trouble. So, open your eyes and see the harm you are inflicting on yourself.

Try the "negative visualization" exercise and make your notes here.

Notes:

____

____

____

____

____

____

____

____

____

On coping with adversity

"Circumstances don't break or make a man, instead, they only reveal your true self."- Epictetus

Winning and losing are two sides of the same coin and so is adversity. It is an undeniable and an inalienable part of your life. You never know when adversity might strike you, but you must understand that you will get through it and that it is just a phase. Like everything else, this too shall pass. Circumstances - both good and bad - don't define your life, but the way you deal with them certainly does. In the face of adversity, you have two options - you can either cower in a corner and complain about how unfair life has been to you, or you can pick yourself up and start doing everything that you can to make it better for yourself. At the end of the day, you are the only one that can control the way you react. So, learn to take everything in your stride, even when things aren't going as you planned.

"Difficulties only strengthen the mind the way physical labor strengthens the body."- Seneca

If you want to become successful in life, then you must develop the strength to overcome adversities as well. The brain is like any other muscle. The way exercising helps strengthen your body physically, adversities are a test for your mental stamina and coping with them strengthens your mind. Overcoming adversity isn't impossible, and it is all about the right attitude. In this section, you will learn about how you can overcome adversity in life.

The right mindset

Your thoughts are important - they are the ones that frame all your successes and failures in life. If you want to overcome adversity in your life, then you must learn to change your belief about challenges. Remember that the quality of your life is not determined by what happens to you, but the way in which you choose to respond to those incidents. The sooner you realize that obstacles weren't designed to prevent you from succeeding, but were placed to help you learn and develop, the easier your life will be. Having a positive mindset is quintessential. A positive mindset is one thing that all successful people have. Did you know that initially, no one was interested in publishing the Harry Potter series written by J.K. Rowling? But she didn't give up, and the rest is history!

Don't make any excuses

We all make excuses when we are too scared of the future. When you make an excuse for something that didn't go the way you expected it to, you fail to see the main reason for that problem. Instead of wasting your energy on coming up with excuses or making excuses, you can spend that time and analyze the problem. For instance, if you made some errors in an important presentation because of your carelessness, the worst thing that you can do in such a situation is to make excuses. When you make an excuse, you fail to see your mistake, this means that chances of you repeating it increase. Instead, if you accept the fact that it was your carelessness that caused the mistakes, you will be doubly careful in the future. Excuses will always limit you, and you cannot overcome adversity if you keep making excuses.

Have some faith

Living a life in fear leeches out more energy than a life that's full of faith. If you fear something, then you will confine yourself to the walls that you put up around yourself. If you have faith, then you can embrace the change. This choice is entirely up to you - you can either live a life in fear or one filled with faith. You must understand that these two things cannot exist simultaneously, and the choice is up to you. Fear can cripple you from moving ahead. However, if you have faith, it will give you the necessary confidence to keep going. For instance, let us assume that you aren't good at public speaking and one fine day, you are supposed to give a speech in front of 500 people. You can either let your fear of public speaking cripple you or you can take a leap of faith and go ahead and deliver the speech. This is a chance that you must take, if you don't try then you will never know.

Never take "no" for an answer

There will be times when your ideas are rejected the same way J.K. Rowling's ideas were rejected, but that doesn't mean that you cower into a corner and let your dreams slip away. If you do this, then you will never be able to achieve anything in life. You must remember that you need to keep trying until you succeed. If you give up the minute you run into any trouble; then you can never fully live your life. Trials are a part of life and whether you endure them or not makes all the difference. Learn never to take no for an answer. Trials are a great way to learn and evolve in life. Learn to bounce back onto your feet and start again. You are the only one that can determine how successful you can be in life and don't let anyone else tell you what you are and aren't. As long as your dreams are practical and attainable, you can achieve them.

Let your success energize you

Failure is as much a part of life as success. You cannot attain success without failing a couple of times. You cannot let the disappointments weigh you down and prevent you from doing something good. You need to keep trying. Whenever you run into any trouble, think of all the troubles that you have overcome in the past. When faced with a difficulty, it might seem like it's the end of the world but remind yourself that you survived it and you will survive this as well. Also, recollect all those instances when you were successful, this will give you the necessary motivation to keep going. As I have mentioned, every failure is a learning opportunity, so learn your lesson and move on. Life can be tricky at times, but it is entirely up to you - the way you deal with adversities.

Try the "voluntary discomfort" exercise and make your notes here.

Notes:

____
____
____

On the art of learning and changing

"Where can I look for good and evil? The answer doesn't lie in the uncontrollable external factors, but within yourself - the choices that you make are your own."- Epictetus

Change is a part of life and learning to cope with change is an invaluable skill. Take a moment and think about it. Are you the same person that you were five years ago? I am certain that you have changed and so did everything around you. Two things that you must never let go of are the willingness to learn and the ability to change. Life is dynamic, so you cannot afford to be stagnant. When you are talking about learning and changing, you must take a look within yourself and consider all the choices that you make.

If you have ever had to move houses or shift from one place to another, then I am certain that you are quite familiar with all the chaos and uncertainty that entails such a move. You might have a hundred questions running through your head about what the new place will be life, if you will like it, how you can commute to work, if you will miss your old place, so on and so forth. A change always affects your psyche, but it is entirely up to you to determine whether it will have a good effect on you or not. Change is always a good thing, and it is a part of life. There are some who find change exhilarating and thrive in it, but then there will be some for whom it is quite scary.

So, why do people fear change?

Uncertainty can be quite scary, and change is a representation of that uncertainty. We all like to know, and when we don't know something, we tend to feel uncomfortable. When you don't know something, there is always scope for surprises (can swing either way) and it also implies that you aren't in control. As soon as "uncertainty" creeps into the picture, we all tend to wobble a little. All the "what if?" questions start creeping in and we struggle with the fact that we aren't in control.

There is one thing about change that is quite fascinating, the more you resist it, the worse you make it for yourself. Also, a lot of people are fine with the changes that they make. Well, change isn't always optional, and at times it is necessary. As mentioned, everyone struggles with change, and once you reach the crossroads (whether to change or not), the worst thing that you can do is fight the change. Resisting any change or putting it off until a later date will only make things worse for you. The harder you try to hold on, the weaker your grasp gets. So, the best thing that you can do is just let go of all your worries and embrace the change. You can either walk along in life, or you can wait for it to drag you along. The pace at which you want to travel is up to you!

This doesn't mean that you must accept every change that comes your way. You are in control, and you can choose what you want to change.

However, once you commit to a change, you must go along with it, and it will open up new opportunities for you. At times, we all tend to spend a lot of time looking backward that we forget about the present. You must always keep an open mind when it comes to change. You must be open to new plans and must not feel too bad when things don't go according to your plan. You must learn to adapt and being adaptable is an important trait in today's world.

Now that I am going on and on about how you need to embrace change, you might wonder why change is good. Well, think of change as a fresh breath of air that will rejuvenate you. Change is good because it is an opportunity to grow and learn. If you stay the same, then you cannot learn, and you certainly cannot grow. Change gives you a chance for growth, and it also helps you learn a little about yourself. It also creates a lot of excitement. Can you imagine how boring your life would be if this world was stagnant and there was no change whatsoever? Predictability is good at times, but leading a predictable life is quite boring. So, change helps keep things exciting and fresh. There is a simple fact that you must accept -

change is an inherent part of life. Everything is in a constant state of change, and nothing ever stays the same. Your wants change, your emotions change, your relationships change, and even our bodies change. When there is so much change going on all around you, what's the point in resisting it? Instead, embrace all this change, and you will feel quite good. It is okay to swim against the tide, but after a while, it can be quite tiresome. So, at times the best thing that you can do is simply let life take its course.

Here are a couple of simple ways in which you can learn to embrace change.

The first thing that you must do is change the way you view "change." Please remember that everything changes constantly and that nothing will ever stay the same. Instead of holding onto your old habits, you need to be proactive and must create new habits for yourself. I don't mean that you must start doing life-changing things right away, but you can certainly start small - like you can make small changes to your attitude. The next time you start to feel a little out of place, see if it is because you are experiencing any uncertainty about it. Usually, we aren't aware that uncertainty is the primary cause of all the anxiety that's associated with change. If uncertainty is the problem, then you must try to change the way you view the situation. Make a list of all the positive aspects associated with the change, and your anxiety will slowly fade away with every positive point you acknowledge.

You must commit to your personal growth. Change is quintessential for growth. Once you embrace any change, you start to learn more about yourself and the way you function. Self-awareness means you can lead a happier and more fruitful life. So, the key to unlocking a better and successful life is to understand the things you must change about yourself.

The final step is to accept change. You must overcome the urge to fight change. Once you do this, you will be pleasantly surprised about how much easier your life will be. Try to not work against it and work with it. Learn to go with the flow, enjoy the present and stop worrying too much about the future. Like the wise old Master Oogway says in Kung Fu Panda "Yesterday is a mystery, tomorrow is a mystery but today is a gift and that's why it is called as the present." Embrace this saying, and you will see a positive change in your life.

Try the "a loan from future" exercise and make your notes here.

Notes:

____
____
____
____
____
____
____
____
___

On clarity and awareness

"What is the reason for all this confusion? It is because nothing seems to be clear and people tend to rely on the most uncertain guide that they can come across - common opinion" - Seneca

When was the last time you took some time for yourself to sit and think about the question that's plagued humanity since time immemorial- "Who am I?" Did you ever make any attempts to see through this fog and try to understand yourself? Having clarity about these questions helps you identify your path in life and helps you stick to it. You must never compare yourself to others. If you do, then please stop doing it immediately. Instead, take this time spent on unnecessary comparison to understand yourself and your life. You cannot let other's opinions to guide your journey, and you must have clarity about who you are and what your purpose in life is. To attain this, you need awareness. When you have clarity and awareness in life, you can choose your battles wisely and will know about the ones that you can avoid. It enables you to fight for all the right reasons and stay away from the wrong ones.

There is an old African saying that goes something like this "The enemies outside cannot harm if there is no enemy within." This essential skill says that self-awareness helps you excel in life. It is one of the essential skills that you need for success. The way you internally process things always govern the way you behave and respond to situations in life. Self-awareness helps you discover any negative thought patterns and behaviors you might have. Once you are aware of all this, you'll be able to make better decisions. In this section, you will learn about the different exercises you can use to improve your self-awareness.

3 Why's

Before you make a decision, you must ask yourself "Why?" once you have your response ask yourself "why" again and then repeat it. You must ask yourself "Why?" thrice before you decide to do something. It will help you obtain the clarity that's necessary to follow through with your actions. If you are self-aware, then you will know your motivation for doing or not doing something, and it helps you determine whether you are reasonable or not. For instance, before you think about shifting your job, ask yourself why? Your reason might be better pay or working hours. Why do you need better pay or working hours? Your answer might be so that you can lead a better life. Ask yourself how earning more money will help you lead a better life? You might say that by earning more, you will be able to provide better for your family or yourself. Now, the final "Why?" will help you find your real motivation for wanting to change your job.

Emotional vocabulary

"The limits of my language mean the limits of my world"- Wittgenstein

Emotions can trigger powerful responses, and they are far more complicated than merely happy and sad. If you can effectively translate your emotions into words, it tends to have a positive effect on your brain. You tend to create stress when you aren't able to articulate your feelings. So, try to label your emotions and the best way to do this is by expanding your emotional vocabulary.

Saying "No."

Being able to say "no" to yourself is a great life skill that helps you ignore any immediate gratification and instead work on a long-term gain that's more fruitful. The ability to say no is much like any other muscle present in your body, and you can strengthen it with a little exercise. For instance, you might want to give up on your diet and binge on a pint of ice cream because you are tempted but doing this will ruin your diet. Instead of giving in to your urge and satisfying a temporary desire, resist it. You will certainly be thankful later for doing this. The more you learn to say no to yourself, the more you can concentrate on the important things in life. It not only helps prioritize things, but it also puts things in perspective. We are all surrounded by temptations - it can be social media, junk food, gossiping or anything. So, make it a daily goal to say "no" to yourself to about five different temptations.

Visceral reactions

All those without self-awareness are merely running on autopilot, and their reactions are involuntary (like knee-jerk reactions). Self-awareness helps you assess a situation rationally and without any bias. If you are caught in a situation that triggers a negative emotion like anger, then you must take a deep breath and calm yourself down. Never react based on what you feel in the moment. If you do this, you give yourself sufficient time to reassess the situation as well as your reaction to it.

Your Flaws

We all have flaws, and no one is "perfect." If you are aware of your flaws, then kudos to you! But your job doesn't end there. You must acknowledge your flaws and also make yourself accountable for them. A lot of people are usually critical to the flaws of others but are unaware of their flaws. Self-awareness helps you analyze yourself and detect any such hypocritical behavior. You can improve yourself only when you realize your flaws and hold yourself accountable for them instead of coming up with excuses.

Self-talk

One of the most damaging things to self-awareness is any form of negative self-talk. Believe it or not, we have a constant commentary going on in our heads, and it isn't usually helpful. Notice the way you react to success as well as failures. If you succeed, do you brush it off as sheer luck? If you fail, do you crucify yourself for it? Your reaction to success and failure creates feedback-loops that are positive and negative. You can be a little tough on yourself, and this will help you perform better in the future. You must, however, balance it with a little compassion. Learn to rejoice in your victories and forgive your failures.

Your body language

Have you ever seen yourself on tape? I am sure it proved to be a rather cringe-worthy experience. Being aware of your body language will improve your self-awareness. If you slouch, a lot of people assume a low-power pose, then it increases cortisol (a stress hormone), and it leads to low self-esteem. When you stand tall or assume a power pose, it makes you feel confident. Learn to use your hand gestures gracefully to articulate your thoughts. The way you talk - your tone, speed, and clarity also determine your self-confidence levels. Watch a couple of videos of skilled speakers and orators and try to imitate their mannerisms.

The Devil's advocate

At times, it is a good idea to take an opposing view about your assumptions. The default views and opinions you have aren't always reasonable or even rational. So, at times, it is a good idea to argue with yourself and check if you are reasonable or not. Also, it is a great workout for your brain. You are your competitor and by indulging in some debate with yourself from time to time will do you some good.

Self-evaluation

Maintain a journal to keep track of your progress. If you were to rate your self-awareness on a scale of one to ten, what will you rate yourself? Think about all the times you say something you regret, repeat any bad habit, make an absent-minded decision or have any erratic thoughts and make a list of all this. You must set some regular goals for yourself - take a big goal of yours and break it up into smaller and more doable goals. Make it a point to ask yourself what are the things that you did well and the things that you must improve upon.

Constructive feedback

All of us tend to have some blind spots when it comes to our behavior and the way we think. If you can obtain constructive feedback regularly, it will help you overcome these blind spots. You might be able to learn a thing or two about yourself that you were previously unaware of. While asking for feedback, only approach those you trust, respect and have your best intentions at heart. It doesn't make any sense to seek feedback from those who want to bring you down or will only say those things that they know that you want to hear.

Another simple exercise that helps you increase your self-awareness is meditation. Start with a ten-minute session and slowly increase the duration of it as you progress.

Improve mental clarity

Here is a simple exercise that you can do to clear your head, calm your mind and free up any blocked mental energy. This activity is referred to as brain dumping. It takes about ten minutes and please try it. The premise of this exercise is quite simple - you must dump all your thoughts on a piece of paper. Here is what you need to do.

The first step is to select a medium. You can either use a paper or open up a fresh document on your laptop. Select a medium according to your convenience and preference.

The next step is to start typing or writing everything that comes to your mind. Yes, I mean write down every thought that crosses your mind. For instance, you might think that the paper looks white and pristine, write it down. If you don't know what to write and are thinking about what to write, write the same thing down - "I am thinking what to write and I don't know." Essentially, you must dump all your thoughts onto the paper. There is no room to overthink anything here, and you don't have to worry about what you write.

Do this for ten to fifteen minutes or for as long as it takes for you to empty your mind. Ten minutes is ideal, but you can go on for as long as you feel like. With this exercise, your writing speed will determine how quickly you can clear your thoughts. If you can write quickly, then you will be able to clear your head quickly. The next time you feel troubled, are unable to focus or are too stressed, then you need to repeat this exercise. It certainly will help you regain your focus. Once your mind feels a little lighter, it is easier to think clearly.

Also, it can be quite interesting to read all that

you note down. Usually, you might notice that most of your thoughts are just all over the place. You might be thinking about eating one moment, and your next thought might be about the project that's due tomorrow. It also helps you understand how your mind processes things. At times you might just come across a brilliant idea! The longer you can do this exercise for, the clearer your mind will be. Of course, it doesn't mean that you stop thinking about a specific thing after you clear your thoughts. You might have 100 thoughts about a certain topic, and this exercise just helped you get rid of ten of those thoughts. You might come across that topic sometime later, and you will end up forming new thoughts about it. Doing this exercise regularly is a good idea because we are all exposed to all sorts of external stimuli regularly and having some mental clarity is quite necessary.

Try the "reflect yourself" exercise and make your notes here.

Notes:

____

____

Chapter 4.2: Mastering your surroundings

On dealing with other people

"The key to keeping good company is to surround yourself with all those people who uplift you and who encourage you to do your best."- Epictetus

Humans are social animals, and that means we interact with a lot of people. We interact with our friends, our family members, colleagues at work and a lot of other people.

"There is only one way in which you can be truly happy, and that's by stopping yourself from worrying about things that are beyond your control."- Seneca

You cannot stop others from being themselves or thinking the way they do, but you can certainly change the way you deal with others around you.

If you want to learn to deal with others effectively, then you must learn the art of diplomacy and here are three steps that will help you along the way.

Never criticize

When you criticize someone, you not only make them defensive but you also unknowingly encourage them to justify their actions or behavior. It is safe to accept that criticism is futile, and it can be quite damaging to someone's pride since it hurts his or her sense of importance. All this will make that person resent you. This holds for all forms of criticism including self-criticism. Criticism makes others feel bad, so refrain from doing it.

Woah, hold on! I am not suggesting that you must never point out their flaws, but you must do it in such a manner that they don't feel discouraged. For instance, if you are pointing out a flaw, ensure that you are coupling it with solutions to overcome the said flaw. Yes, solutions - if possible, always suggest alternate solutions so that the person still feels like they are in control.

Always keep the age-old adage that "You can catch more flies with honey instead of vinegar." So, if you are trying to win over others while staying true to yourself, then you need to try using subtle persuasion and appreciation instead of a head-on confrontation.

Be appreciative

Who likes it when their ideas, suggestions or even work is rejected? No one does! Genuine appreciation is quite welcome. I don't mean that you must resort to unnecessary flattery, but everyone likes it when they are appreciated for a job that's done well. It can be something as simple as acknowledging their efforts or even saying thank you.

Appreciation must be frequent - in public as well as in private. It doesn't take long to appreciate someone, but it certainly goes a long way. It helps make the other person feel valued, appreciated and even confident. I am sure when you say thank you to someone for their efforts, it certainly puts a smile on their face.

Other's perspective

If you can place yourself in the other person's shoes, even for a moment, you will be able to gain some perspective. You will be able to see the entire picture better, and it enables you to display genuine concern. At times, all that someone needs is for his or her perspective to be seen and heard. Well, stoicism helps with this.

Try the "Forgive Other's Wrongs" exercise and make your notes here.

Notes:

____

____

____

____

____

____

____

____

On thinking what others think

"All that we hear are mere opinions and aren't facts. Everything that we see is our perspective, and that's not necessarily the truth."- Aurelius

The first thing that you must understand is that you never really know what someone else is thinking or feeling. You merely know what they tell you. So, you must not let such opinions or beliefs dictate your life. If someone has something nice to say, take it in your stride and if they don't, then ignore it.

"If someone tells you that a specific person is speaking ill of you, then don't make any excuses about what is being said. Instead, your answer must be 'he was ignorant of my other flaws, else he might not have mentioned the ones he did.'"- Epictetus

People talk, that's their job. There will be someone or another who thinks that you aren't doing something right or that you are a flawed human being. Well, you cannot control what others think, but you can certainly decide about letting things affect you.

Everyone wants to feel like they are accepted, and this is quite natural. Humans survive better in groups, and the need to feel like you belong to one is a human instinct. In this section, you will learn about a couple of different things that you can use while learning to deal with what others think. It is all about creating a new mindset to maintain healthy relationships with yourself as well as those around you.

Perspective

People will care less about what others think about them if they are aware of how little others think about them. This is true. We all have sufficient things to keep ourselves occupied. Everyone has his or her own set of insecurities to cope with. So, if you worry about how others perceive well, let me tell you something - others worry about the same thing too!

Question yourself

Cognitive distortions coupled with negative thinking will certainly affect your mood and behavior. Most of us tend to be fixated on finding the bad in every situation and assume the worst while ignoring all the good in it. We tend to overanalyze things and jump to unnecessary and dire conclusions. So, the next time you feel like any such thoughts are creeping in, the first thing you must do is stop yourself and start questioning such false beliefs you are forming.

Perfectionism

It might be quite hard to let go of the feeling that you must do things the "right" way or else you won't be liked, accepted or even admired. This is nothing more than a colossal waste of your time and effort. Perfection is nothing more than an illusion, and no such thing exists. So, let go of your need for perfection and instead try to do things that you do enjoy.

Understand yourself

What are your likes? What do you want? Are all the choices that you make solely based on your wants or are you doing it to impress others? Permit yourself to try new things regardless of what others think. After all, it is your life, and if you want to make the most of it, then you must start living it the way you want.

Your tribe

There will be people who appreciate and accept you for who you are. You don't have to waste your time trying to fit in. Try to be your authentic and genuine self, and you will find others who are like you. So, you must try to accept yourself and stop doing or acting in a certain fashion so that others will accept you.

Vulnerabilities

Going against the grain or taking a risk can be quite scary. However, what matters is that you must trust yourself and take the first step. You cannot grow in life if you keep playing safe. You must escape your safety net and allow yourself to stumble and fall to grow. You cannot learn if you don't try.

You must learn to be your friend. Make peace with yourself and who you are. You don't have to put on a façade by conforming to the societal standards if you don't want to! You don't have to worry about what others think or believe about you. You know your worth and don't let anyone else tell you otherwise.

Try the "instead, buy some tranquility" exercise and make your notes here.

Notes:

____

____

____

____

____

____

____

____

____

On seeking fame

"You don't have to seek good in the external things, instead seek it within yourself."- Epictetus

Who doesn't want fame and glory? We are all constantly searching for the elusive fame. What is fame? Does fame mean a huge bank balance or driving in the best cars? Well, fame is quite subjective, and there is nothing wrong in seeking it. However, in this process, one must not lose sight of themselves. It is okay to see good in all external things, but don't forget about yourself. Take a hard look at your life and instead of jumping into the rat race, try to stand apart from the crowd. A person who is not happy with himself or herself will be miserable regardless of all the fame that they achieve.

Fame and fortune are fickle as well as mysterious. What makes one person wealthy and famous while the rest of his entourage is left behind? Most of us want to become rich and famous. We are either open about it or harbor a secret desire for the same. So, what makes the rich and famous different from the rest? Here are a couple of life hacks that are based on Stoic philosophy and will help you see life differently.

You must always focus your time and attention on things that are important. Instead of squandering away these precious resources on doing things and tasks that don't matter, learn to do things that you enjoy and will bring you a step closer to your goal.

You can aim for perfection, but the rich and famous know that it is okay to settle for excellence. If you aim for the stars, you will land on the moon. This is a brilliant thought. It not only encourages you to do better in life and push yourself, but it also helps you be satisfied with the results that you obtain. Your integrity is one of the most precious things you own, and you must never let it breakdown.

Learn to take calculated risks. Risks are essential for growth, and they push you out of your comfort zone. Only when you leave your safety net will you be able to grow. However, learn to take calculated risks and don't expose yourself to excessive risk.

Learn to make your own rules. When you make your set of rules, others will need to play according to them, and you are in control - at least to a certain extent. This doesn't mean breaking any laws. It merely means that you must try to push the limits whenever possible.

Try to give more than you take. No one likes to be around a person who constantly preys on others or takes advantage of those around them. You must strive to offer greater value than you take and you will notice that more people will want to work with you.

Learn to manage your resources - especially time and effort. You can control what you use these resources for, and they aren't unlimited. So, prioritize in life and work on those things that are important to you. When you like what you do, you will automatically dedicate 100% of all that you have to work at hand, and that's the key to success.

Try the "always count your blessings" exercise and make your notes here.

Notes:

____

____

____

____

____

____

____

____

___

On virtue and kindness

"When it is genuine and devoid of any hypocrisy, kindness is truly invincible. What harm can even the most malicious of souls inflict on you when you show them sincere kindness and if given a chance, you point out where they went wrong?"- Aurelius

You must accept the fact that you will come across people who are rude in your life. It happens daily. Someone might cut you in line, someone might speak to others like they are inferior to them, people might lie and take credit for the work that you did and so on. Not only is all this common, but I am sure that this has happened to you at some point or another. There will be times when there are no consequences to such rude acts of others.

They might have to wait for a shorter duration in line than you; they might get the promotion that you were working for by taking credit for your efforts. When you see all this, you might get angry, plot a way to extract revenge or even resent them. These are the emotions that a person might experience. You must understand that a stoic will never react in such a manner. None of the above-mentioned reactions will reduce their rude behavior.

As Aurelius said, "You can always hold your breath until you turn blue, but they are still going to keep doing it."

So, how does a stoic respond to such selfish behavior?

Don't take it personally

The first thing that is abundantly clear to a stoic is that one must not take it personally since it wasn't anything personal. Marcus Aurelius once wrote to himself to not be irritated with the way people smell or their bad breath. What is the point of getting irritated at it? They certainly aren't doing it on purpose, and if a human being has armpits or a mouth, then they are bound to smell at one point or another. The same logic applies to a person who was selfish. We all have those behavioral traits in us, and it can bother some people at times. Whenever Aurelius encountered a difficult or a shameless person, he would ask himself "Is it possible to live in a world without any shamelessness? The answer is no. So, don't ask for the impossible. There will be some shameless people in this world, and this happens to be one of them."

Has it harmed you?

Whenever a stoic expresses any form of rudeness, they usually ask themselves if such rudeness has harmed them somehow. If someone calls you an ugly name or talks to you in a tone that's rude, did it harm you in any way? No, it didn't, and it is all in your head. You must remember that no one can do you any harm unless you let them. If someone talks ill about you, it will affect you only if you allow it to affect you. If you don't, then they are just words that hold no true meaning. You know what you are and aren't, don't let others be the judge of you.

Don't respond to rudeness

Responding to rudeness in kind will not do you any good. A stoic will always resist the temptation to do this. A stoic will not hate a hater and will certainly not treat a jerk like a jerk, even if the said person is a jerk. The best way to avenge yourself is by not stopping to their level. It is better to heal from any injury than seek revenge for it and vengeance is nothing more than a colossal wastage of your time, and it merely makes you vulnerable for more injuries. So, the best response in such a situation is to not extract any revenge, in fact doing this is the best revenge you can get. If someone is rude to you and you respond rudely to them, then you haven't done anything other than proving to them that their actions were justified. If you respond to someone's dishonesty by being dishonest to them, guess what you have just proved? You just proved them right, and now everyone is dishonest.

Taking the high road is the best response when you are facing any unpleasantness. Even the bible says that one must be nice and caring even to their most hateful enemy. Hatred is the expected reaction to hatred and kindness is unusual. So, if someone is mean to you today, respond to them kindly and be the bigger person. This isn't a reaction that they might expect, and it will even embarrass them. You aren't stooping to their level but are trying to bring them up to yours.

So, it is a good idea to be better and not let others hurt or disappoint you. You must strive to be the example that others will want to follow. It is quite terrible to cheat, to be selfish and to inflict suffering on others. Instead, living your life morally is a better option. Also, most people use rudeness or meanness to mask some deep-seated weakness of theirs. Kindness has great strength to it, have the courage to use it.

Try the "forgive other's wrongs" exercise and make your notes here.

Notes:

____

____

____

____

____

____

____

____

____

On money and wealth

"Wealth isn't only about having all material possessions; true wealth is having limited wants."- Epictetus

Wants are certainly unlimited. You might wish for something now, and once you have it, you will start wishing for something else. There is no end to your wants. So, the greatest wealth in life is not having all sorts of materialistic possessions you desire, but in having fewer wants. Wants tend to create a lot of stress. Once a want is fulfilled, then some other want will replace it, and this cycle never ends until you make a conscious decision to put an end to it.

In this section, you will learn about developing certain daily patterns that will help you find success in life. Don't measure success in terms of money or wealth; both of these things are quite meaningless in the end. Acquiring materialistic possessions doesn't make you wealthy. Instead, learning to lead a life that feels fruitful and tranquil is the real success!

Daily good habits

The primary difference between all those who are successful and those who don't boil down to their daily habits. Successful people have plenty of good habits and only a few bad ones. Try to understand that your bad habits get in the way of your success and prevent you from realizing your true potential. Take a sheet of paper and make two columns. In one column, make a list of all your bad habits or what you think are bad habits and in the other column, invert each of the bad habits and reframe them as good habits. For instance, if you spend too much time watching television, it's a bad habit. Now, let us reframe it as a good habit – 'I only watch TV for an hour daily.'

Create goals

If you fail to plan, then you are planning to fail! If you want to turn things around for yourself, then you must strive to create regular goals for yourself. The goals that you set for yourself must be small, measurable, realistic and time-bound. Once you set these goals for yourself, develop a plan of action to achieve them. You can perhaps take one positive step per day to move a step closer to your goals. Also, keep track of your progress so that you are aware of the areas in which you are lagging.

Self-improvement

You must constantly try to think of different ways in which you can improve yourself. There is no ceiling limit to your personal growth. It can be something as simple as reading about different things or trying out new activities. Also, learn to not spend your time on activities that aren't important to you. Make a list of three of the most important goals in your life and pick one of them. If something doesn't help you attain that goal, then it is a waste of your time.

Your health matters

Your health is your greatest resource. Only if you are healthy will you be able to attain anything in life. So, please don't ignore your health and instead learn to take care of yourself.

Eating healthily, exercising regularly and getting sufficient sleep are three simple ways in which you can improve your health! When you are healthy, you will be energetic and focused, and all this helps you work harder on achieving your goals.

Relationships matter

It can be quite lonely on top. So, you must ensure that you focus on the relationships in your life as well. Spending time with people you love and those who genuinely love you is a wonderful feeling. It will make you feel refreshed and energized. Also, it is a great way to network.

Moderation

There must be moderation in every aspect of your life and in all things that you do. It simply means that you must always have a balanced approach to your work, eating habits, exercise routine and everything else. When you do things in moderation, you will be able to focus on things that are important to you without burning yourself out.

Get things done

Your biggest enemy is procrastination, and you must avoid putting things off for later. You must get things done and get them done right away! The more you procrastinate, the chances of you getting around to doing it will fade away. Make a list of three important things that you must get done daily, and these things must take a step closer to your goals. Regardless of all that you do, please ensure that you do those three tasks that you set for yourself.

Positivity

Winning and losing is a part of life. At times you might come out on top, and at times you might fail spectacularly. All this is a part of life, and they are unavoidable. There is one thing that you can do regardless of all that comes your way, and that's to maintain a positive attitude. If you have a positive attitude toward things in life, then nothing can bring you down. You will find an opportunity even in the bleakest of times when you stay positive. Also, positivity attracts more positivity. You must not indulge in any negative self-thinking. It is okay to be critical of yourself from time to time, but don't just focus on it at all times!

Try the "A loan from future" exercise and make your notes here.

Notes:

____

____

____

____

____

____

____

____

____

On luxurious living

"A person who has too little isn't poor, but the man who craves for a lot more is."- Seneca

Living a luxurious life doesn't mean having all the finest things in life. There will be no end to all the materialistic things that you might want. There is no end to this craving. Not being able to satisfy yourself is the worst feeling ever. If you don't learn to be content with what you have, you will never be content in life. A person who cannot find this sense of contentedness is truly poor regardless of his or her financial status.

It is quite easy to live a luxurious life, and it doesn't mean living large! A couple of simple changes are all that you must make to your daily routine to ensure that you are breaking free of any bad habits and to learn that it is okay to make yourself a priority, to lead a life that's full of freedom, good relationships, and quality products. This is what a luxurious life is all about.

Your schedule

We all lead extremely hectic lives these days and are quite drained out by the end of the day. Try to eliminate one thing from your schedule that you don't have to do and instead make time for something that you do like. Maybe you like to paint or sketch, so instead of watching TV for an hour daily, use this time to work on your painting or drawing skills! It will not only make you feel happy, but it is a great stress buster as well.

Don't forget to schedule regular breaks for yourself. If you don't take regular breaks, you will burn yourself out sooner or later.

Go tech-free

Every month make it a point to spend at least one day away from all your electronic gadgets! Yes, no mobile phones, computers, laptops or tablets. Give yourself some time to clear your mind and learn to live in the moment. This will give you some perspective about your life!

Bad habits

Breaking free of bad habits might not necessarily seem like a luxury, but it is one of the best things you can do to improve the quality of your life. When you overcome a bad habit, it gives you a certain sense of confidence and accomplishment. Not just that, but it will also make you feel like you are in control. It doesn't necessarily have to be a serious vice; it can be something as simple as resisting the temptation to binge on any junk food or starting to make your bed every morning.

Buy something

Minimalism is an important part of stoicism. Make a list of things that you need and buy one of those items. Ensure that it is something that you will regularly use and is not easily replaceable. Try to aim for quality over quantity while making the purchase.

Healthy living

A healthy lifestyle is truly luxurious. Leading a life that is healthy and isn't toxic has become quite rare these days. It means that you must get rid of everything that is toxic for your growth and this list includes toxic relationships as well. Try to improve the quality of your life by making time for meaningful things and relationships and get rid of everything that is toxic.

Try the "Instead, buy some tranquility" exercise and make your notes here.

Notes:

____

____

____

____

____

____

____

____

____

Chapter 4.3: Facing the Evening of Life

On becoming old

"To desire nothing replaces pleasure. How good does it feel to be tired of wanting and to leave it all behind?"- Seneca

This is one piece of ancient Stoic philosophy that's quite useful in today's world. It certainly comes in handy when learning to deal with old age. To want nothing and to see the pleasure in desiring nothing is quite the opposite of the way the modern society is fueled by consumerism functions. These days, we are constantly bombarded with the notion that one should always desire more and the only way to be happy is by acquiring more. The modern-day consumerist philosophy is to want, buy, acquire and spend more to find happiness and satisfaction. Stoics say that we have got it all wrong, and it does make sense.

In today's world, being youthful is glorified whereas growing older is seen as something that must be avoided. However, as you grow old, it doesn't mean that the quality of your life needs to decrease.

Growing old is a natural process, and you must accept it. Here are a couple of tips that you can follow to develop the right mindset about growing old.

Set realistic expectations

The popular Bryan Adam's song "18 till I die" is about staying young at heart even as you grow old. Our present culture is all about encouraging people to think that they can stay young forever if they use the right creams, take care of their bodies and take the necessary supplements. The fact is all of these aren't true. So, it is a good idea to have some realistic expectations about aging. For instance, if you think that you can keep doing everything that you did while in your 20's when you are in your 60's is an unrealistic expectation. You can stay young at heart, but you must accept that your body will grow old and you might not be able to do everything as you used to and it is okay.

Relax a little

A lot of people tend to panic when they realize that they are growing old. The result of this is a fight or flight response that makes them seek a miracle cure. Instead, try to maintain your calm and positively take everything. This is the time for some sober introspection. It helps you accept all the changes instead of resisting it and helps you find happiness regardless of the stage of your life.

Don't be in denial

Trying to look and feel good as you age is not wrong. However, growing old doesn't mean that you must hide your age from yourself or those around you. If eating right and using the right products makes your skin look youthful, then that's good. But don't be in denial that you aren't growing old. Clinging to any unnecessary physical illusions leads to denial and living in denial means that you forget about your life.

Attractiveness

Being attractive isn't limited to just external beauty. Don't forget that beauty is just skin deep, and it will fade away. So, clinging on to it doesn't make any sense. Being self-assured, happy, active, and confident are attractive traits regardless of your age. So, work on developing these traits instead of holding on to any futile notions about beauty and attractiveness.

Don't live in your past

Your past must stay in the past. Learn to embrace it but don't live in it. If you spend your time in the past, you forget about the time that you do have. Instead, learn to make the most of that time. Reflect on your past, cherish your memories but don't try to relive it. It is all done, and it belongs where it is, in the past. For instance, a sense of nostalgia might prompt you to play football, go ahead and do it. But keep in mind that you might not be able to play like you used to and make peace with it.

Be proud and grateful

Be grateful for all the experiences you had and be proud of the person they've made you become. The fact that you are growing old means that you have survived everything that life dished out. The life experiences you had have taught you some valuable lessons and accept it all. It has given you certain wisdom that only comes with age, rejoice it. Your perspective in life is different because of all that you endured, pat yourself on the back. After all, age is just a number, and you must not fear it.

Try the "love your fate" exercise and make your notes here.

Notes:

____

____

____

____

____

On losing control

"The most important task in life is to be able to identify and differentiate matters in which you have a say from the things that you cannot control. Then where can one look for good and evil in this world? You don't have to look at all the external circumstances that you cannot control but must peek at yourself and the choices that you can make."- Epictetus

The most important aspect of Stoic philosophy is the ability to differentiate between the things that you can and cannot control. What are the things that you can and cannot influence? If your flight is canceled due to bad weather conditions, regardless of all the shouting at an airline manager, the flight will still stay canceled. It doesn't matter how much you wish for it; you will not be born taller, shorter or be born on a different continent. Regardless of how hard you try, you cannot make someone else love you. All the time that you spend on trying to control and change things that are clearly beyond your control will only lead to dissatisfaction and irritation.

One of the most common fears that people have is the thought of losing control. This is the fear that if you cannot control something, then it will lead to something bad. All this is a source of stress and anxiety. The world is an uncertain place, and you cannot control everything. The only thing that you can control is the way you respond to situations, but that's about it. You cannot control the future because it is unpredictable and believing otherwise is sheer foolishness. Here are a couple of ways in which you can stop worrying about all the things you cannot control.

What can you control?

The reality of life is that there are plenty of things that you cannot control. You cannot control the way people act, behave or think, you cannot control the outcome of things and you certainly cannot control any external events. Instead of stressing about all the things you cannot control, think about the things you can control. You can control your attitude, the way you think and the effort you make. When you focus on the things you can control, you will stop worrying about everything else.

Your Fears

We all have various worst-case scenarios in our heads, and the usual outcomes aren't nearly as dire as we imagined. Most people are usually busy worrying and thinking, "This is going to be such a disaster" that they don't take the time to think, "What will I do if the worst-case scenario does come true?" Perhaps you will need to struggle for a while, but the chances are that you are strong enough to keep going. You must acknowledge your fears and come up with ways in which you can overcome those fears.

Your influence

You certainly cannot make things go your way, but you do have some influence. So, you cannot make your child be a great student, but you can certainly provide the child with the necessary tools to do his or her best. You cannot force someone to have fun, but you can create an environment that's conducive of fun. To exert influence, you must be in control of your attitude. If you have any concerns about someone else's choices, then express your opinion and maybe offer an alternative course of action, but you cannot force them to do something you want.

Contemplation vs. problem-solving

Rethinking about yesterday's actions in your head and dwelling on the disastrous consequences isn't useful, but problem solving is. So, ask yourself if you are merely ruminating or if you are trying to solve a problem. Try to actively seek solutions instead of thinking of ways in which you can completely avoid the problems. Problems are a part of life and preparing yourself to deal with them is better than to think that you can avoid them. If you start ruminating, immediately acknowledge that all those thoughts in your head aren't helping you in any manner and are a waste of time.

Healthy affirmations

We entertain over 70,000 thoughts per day, that's about 3000 thoughts in an hour! Woah that's a lot of thinking. Most of these thoughts tend to be negative - related to self-doubt, fear, anxiety and discouragement. Always keep a couple of healthy affirmations handy. Whenever you notice a negative thought creeping up, replace it with a positive thought. You can control the way you think, so changing your attitude in life is the key to leading a happy and successful life.

You cannot control the way you age or how you age. At times, you might forget where you have placed your car keys because you were concentrating on something else. Then when you need to go out, you cannot find your keys and a tiny inner voice says "You are getting old and that's making you forgetful."

Well, stop yourself immediately! That's nothing more than a negative thought! You must rethink and rephrase that internal dialogue. You were probably focusing on something else and this made you place the keys in a location without paying any heed to it. It doesn't mean that you are forgetful; it simply means that you were distracted.

If you have any inner mental dialogue about how aging makes you lose control, you must replace all of that with positive affirmation. You must remind yourself that aging isn't something that you can control. However, it doesn't mean that you can no longer live your life the way you want to!

Try the "voluntary discomfort" exercise and make your notes here.

Notes:

____

____

____

____

On facing mortality

"I will die, then must I lament about dying and die lamenting? If I were to be put in chains, must I lament then? If I were to be exiled, then can anyone prevent me from going into exile with a smile on my face?"- Epictetus

There are only two things that are certain in life - taxes and death. You can delay them for a while, but they are certainly impossible to avoid. You cannot cheat death, but you can certainly determine the way you want to go out! The sooner you accept your mortality, the more peace you will be at. Human life is quite fragile, and you must come to terms with it. Accepting your mortality will help you put things in perspective, and you will be able to concentrate on the things that you do enjoy instead of squandering your time on things and people who don't matter.

There are certain things that you can do to make peace with your mortality, and they are as follows.

Paperwork

Do you have all the necessary legal documents like a will that will give your dear ones the instructions they need to deal with all the stuff that you leave behind? Do you have a will that will help your dear ones make any medical decisions on your behalf? This might seem quite grim, but it will certainly help you come to terms with your mortality. It helps relieve some anxiety and will be helpful to your loved ones later on.

Mindfulness

You need some emotional and spiritual acceptance to fully embrace your mortality.

Thinking or obsessing about death isn't healthy, but you can use mindfulness to get used to that idea, and it helps reduce any anxiety you experience. Take some time for yourself and come to terms with your mortality. It helps you resolve any unresolved feelings you might have about death. Once you do this, you will notice that you are calmer than before.

Discuss death

Death is one topic that no one likes to talk about. It is inevitable, and it is better to talk about it instead of pretending that it isn't real. The way you discuss politics, talk about death too. I don't mean that you must constantly discuss it, but talking about it will prepare others around you as well. After all, mortality isn't something that's specific only to you. Your loved ones need to make peace with it as well.

Good death

You certainly don't have any choice about when and how you die, but there are some decisions that you can make about how you want to spend the last years of your life. Try to visualize what a good death means to you? Don't wait until the last moment to think about it and instead do it immediately. Spend some time thinking about the sights, people, location and tastes you want when you die.

Try the exercise on "self-reflection" and make your notes here.

Notes:

____

____

____

____

____

____

____

____

____

On acceptance

"You must not act like you are going to live forever. Death is something that looms over our heads. While you live and when it is in your power, try to be good."- Aurelius

You must accept the fact that you will grow old sooner or later. It isn't avoidable, and you cannot escape it. Learn to make your peace with this fact, and you will be able to reduce some stress. Since our time on this earth is limited, try to make the most of it and try to be good to yourself and those around you.

Acceptance can change your life, but it isn't an easy concept to understand. Acceptance isn't a cognitive function, and it is more of a bodily process that takes some while to be fully processed and understood. The one thing that you must do is forget about non-acceptance to embrace acceptance.

Accepting yourself and the things around you the way they are can bring you a lot of peace. Acceptance comes with time, and it isn't something that you can learn instantly. It takes some time and contemplation. Whatever has happened is in the past and accept it. If you don't like something, you can try to make amends, but that's all that you can do - make peace with this fact as well.

Try the "count your blessings" exercise and make your notes here.

Notes:

____

____

____

____

____

____

____

____

___

On meditation

"Look within - there lies your source of strength that will keep you going. You merely need to look for it."- Aurelius

Meditation is the best way to understand yourself. You don't have to depend on anyone for your happiness or to derive strength to keep going. You are self-sufficient, and all that you must do is look within. Meditation is the best means to do this.

If you meditate daily, you will find a positive change in your mental abilities. When you feel at peace and relaxed, you can think better and make better decisions. Your mental functions will improve, that is your cognitive skills will be stronger. You don't have to meditate for years together to achieve the benefits of meditation. Even contemplating daily for eight weeks will have a positive impact on your life. A human brain is a complex machine. However, it doesn't mean that it is free of any form of influence. The mind is like any other muscle in the body, and it can be trained. If you exercise regularly, you can build muscle or tone your body. In the same manner, regular meditation can help in improving your brain's health.

Meditation improves your awareness. Awareness comes from concentration. When you are aware, you can notice things that you usually don't. For instance, if you are a fish, you wouldn't be aware of water, would you? If you want to understand water, then the fish needs to go outside its "usual" element. That is precisely the core objective of meditation. It is about stepping out of your usual part to become aware of the reality.

When you meditate, you can control your thoughts instead of your thoughts controlling you. When you can focus on one thing instead of all the million things going around you, you can think clearly. Can you make the right decision when you are feeling quite emotional or restless? For instance, if you fight with your spouse, can you concentrate on the work you are doing? Perhaps not. Your mind will try to discern the reason for the fight on a subconscious level. The trick to better decision-making is being present in the moment. If you think about the past or worry about the future, you possibly cannot make the right decision about your present.

Try the "self-reflection" exercise or meditate for a while and make your notes here.

Notes:

____

____

____

____

____

____

____

____

____

Conclusion

I want to thank you once again for choosing this book, and I hope it proved to be an enjoyable and an entertaining read.

We all live in a world of chaos, and if you want to retain some tranquility, then you need Stoicism. It is a simple philosophy that helps you concentrate on the important things in life and help you lead a fruitful life.

There are different Stoic exercises mentioned in this book that will help you embrace the Stoic lifestyle. As with any change, it takes a while to embrace this lifestyle fully. It will take some time, so you must be patient and consistent in your efforts if you want to reap all the benefits that it offers.

Follow the exercises and make your notes as you go along. It helps you keep track your progress and work on yourself. Now, all that's left for you to do is get started as soon as possible!

Thank you and all the best!

www.ingramcontent.com/pod-product-compliance
Lightning Source LLC
La Vergne TN
LVHW020336200726

843507LV00012B/2383